PHYSICAL
SCIENCE
PROJECTS
★ for kids ★

A PROJECT GUIDE TO

LIGHT

AND

OPTICS

Colleen Kessler

Mitchell Lane

P.O. Box 196
Hockessin, Delaware 19707
Visit us on the web: www.mitchelllane.com
Comments? email us: mitchelllane@mitchelllane.com

Mitchell Lane

PHYSICAL SCIENCE PROJECTS
☆ for kids ☆

A Project Guide to:
Chemistry • Electricity and Magnetism
Forces and Motion • **Light and Optics**
Matter • Sound

Printing 1 2 3 4 5 6 7 8 9

Copyright © 2012 by Mitchell Lane Publishers

All rights reserved. No part of this book may be reproduced without written permission from the publisher. Printed and bound in the United States of America.

Library of Congress
Cataloging-in-Publication Data
Kessler, Colleen.
 A project guide to light and optics / Colleen D. Kessler.
    p. cm. — (Physical science projects for kids)
 Includes bibliographical references and index.
 ISBN 978-1-58415-969-8 (lib. bd.)
 1. Light—Experiments—Juvenile literature.
 2. Optics—Experiments—Juvenile literature.
 3. Science projects—Juvenile literature. I. Title.
 QC360.K47 2011
 535—dc22

                                          2011000720
eBook ISBN: 9781612281117

                                          PLB

CONTENTS

INTRODUCTION

Optics is the study of light—what it is, where it comes from, and why it behaves like it does—but the science deals with more than just lighting. From torches to lasers, optics has led humans to many amazing discoveries. Electronics such as CDs and DVDs, personal music players, and more have come about because of optics.

Without light, there would be no sight. Imagine walking into your bedroom at night from a dark hallway. The curtains are drawn, and it is pitch black. You can't see anything. Does that mean that your room has suddenly become empty? No, all of your belongings are still there—you just can't see them.

You are able to see because of light. When light from an object reaches your eyes, your eyes signal your brain. You understand the appearance and location of that object.

Some objects are luminous—they create their own light. The stars are luminous objects. A lit lamp is another. Other objects are illuminated—they reflect light from another source. The Moon is an illuminated object. Your kitchen table is another.

Light moves in a predictable way. It travels in a straight line from the source to whatever it is illuminating. When it reaches that object, the light is reflected. Light can also be refracted, which means turned or bent. At least as early as 165 CE, people were learning how light is refracted. Archaeologists have discovered evidence that ancient

An example of how light moves in a straight line can be seen at a laser light show concert.

Egyptians may have used lenses to correct vision and may have even had telescopes powerful enough to see far into space. At the very least, these ancient people had found methods for grinding perfectly convex and concave pieces of glass.

Other ancient cultures studied the way light behaves as well.

Concave Lens

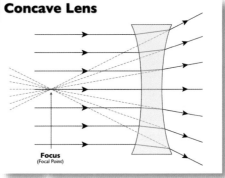

Focus
(Focal Point)

Convex Lens

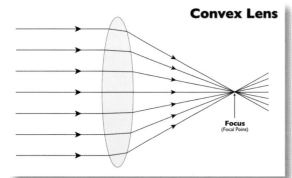

Focus
(Focal Point)

Ancient Greeks held many theories about how light worked. Plato (c. 428–c.348 BCE) believed that human eyes emit light. He couldn't explain, though, why humans could not see in dark places. Ibn al Haytham (c.965–c.1040) an Arab astronomer who is also known as Alhazen, published *The Book of Optics*. In all of his work, he followed the scientific method, proving his theories with verifiable data. He included detailed descriptions of the laws of reflection and refraction.

Around 1600, German scientist Johannes Kepler (1571–1630) described how curved lenses could bend light to improve eyesight. The curved lens of the eye focuses light on the retina at the back of the eye. Sometimes the eye lens is curved more or less than it should be, and images are blurred. Adding eyeglasses changes how the light enters the eye and corrects imperfect vision.

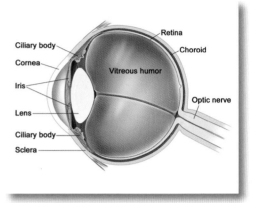

Diagram of the human eye

Benjamin Franklin (1706–1790) later improved the design of eyeglasses. He invented bifocals, which have two sets of lenses for each eye. One bends the light to help focus on things that are close up. The other bends light to help focus on things that are far away.

Benjamin Franklin's bifocals

Scientists also invented telescopes for viewing outer space. By using two refracting lenses in a tube, Galileo Galilei (1564–1642) improved the telescope to see farther than ever before into the solar system.

Light is also used to view tiny objects. The microscope uses refractive lenses to magnify small objects. Englishman Robert Hooke (1635–1703) described what he saw with a compound microscope in 1665. The microscope allowed him to see colors in soap bubbles and flakes of mica.

Robert Hooke's microscope

Galileo Demonstrating His Telescope, Venice, 1609 (Louis Figuier, 1870). In this artist's reconstruction, Galileo is showing his telescope to the Doge and the Venetian Senators. Galileo is credited with making the first effective telescope.

In the late 1600s, English physicist Isaac Newton (1642–1727) proved that white light is actually made up of many colors. He sent a beam of light through a glass prism. The prism separated the light, making a rainbow of colors called a spectrum.

Newton continued to experiment with light. He showed that light is made up of tiny particles. (Later scientists would call these particles photons). The particles are too small to see individually. They have no mass, and they move very fast. He also developed the theory that light travels in straight lines.

Christiaan Huygens (1629–1695), a Dutch physicist, disagreed. He said that photons may behave like particles in some ways, but they

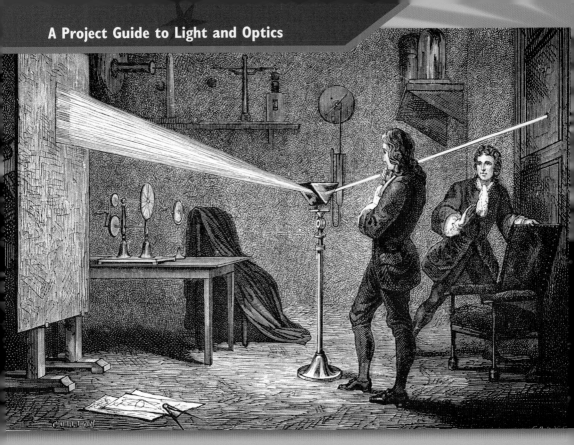

Engraving of Sir Isaac Newton performing an optics experiment with a prism. Newton (at center) passed a ray of light through a prism in a dark room onto a screen. The white light was refracted (bent) but different parts of it were refracted to a different extent. The screen was illuminated by bands of consecutive colors of the spectrum: red, orange, yellow, green, blue, indigo, and violet.

move like waves. Two hundred years later, Scottish physicist James Clerk Maxwell (1831–1879) agreed that it travels in waves. He also believed that it is electrical in nature, not mechanical, like sound. In 1860, he published his theory that light is electromagnetic.

Since then, as technology has developed, a range of waves has been discovered and used, including X-rays, television signals, and radio waves. The range is called the electromagnetic spectrum.

Scientists continued to try to figure out whether light is made of particles or waves. Through the work of Max Planck (1858–1947), Albert Einstein (1879–1955), and others, a new idea grew—that all matter has the properties of both particles and waves.

About forty years later, in 1960, Light Amplification by Stimulated Emission of Radiation—or *laser*—was invented. Like many new ideas, people laughed at its value. Today, lasers are used to read and burn CDs, carve precise grooves in machinery, check out purchases at department stores, provide wireless interfacing between video game consoles and controllers, perform innovative surgeries, and guide aircraft in for safe landings.

The study of optics has come far since the first Greek and Arab scholars began to formulate how light worked. In this book, you'll learn more about the properties of light. You'll investigate how it travels, bends, bounces, and changes speed. You'll see how it is made up of many colors, and where it falls on the electromagnetic spectrum.

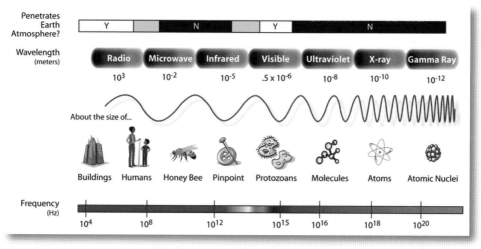

Electromagnetic Spectrum

Before starting any activity, read the instructions all the way through, and work with an adult when the activity asks you to do so. You may want to keep a science notebook as a record of your journey through the activities in this book. This will allow you to look back, improve upon your methods, and replicate the activities and experiments to see if they turn out the same way. In this way, you can expand the projects for science fair experiments.

By the time you finish the activities in this book, you will have a greater understanding of what light can do. You may even follow in the footsteps of the amazing scientists who taught us what we know about optics, and make new and bigger discoveries.

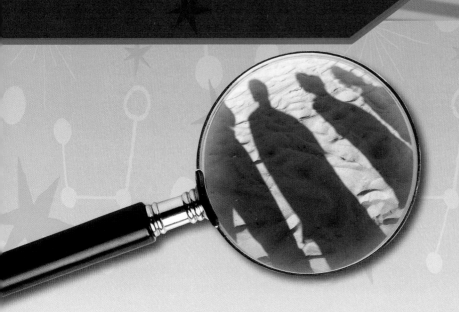

LINES OF LIGHT

Do you see shadows when you walk outside on a sunny day? These shadows are evidence that light travels in straight lines. Shadows are made when an object does not let light pass through it. The object absorbs or reflects the light, leaving a shadow on the other side.

In this activity, you'll use a comb to block rays of light. Observe the shadows. Does the comb block the flashlight rays in the same way that a tree blocks the sun's rays?

Materials
- A room that can be darkened
- Hole punch
- Dark-colored card stock
- Comb
- Masking tape
- Flashlight

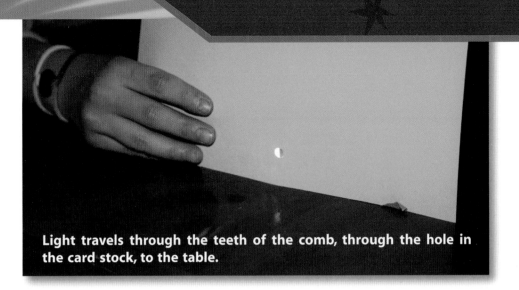

Light travels through the teeth of the comb, through the hole in the card stock, to the table.

Instructions

1. Use a hole punch to make a hole in a piece of card stock along one of the long edges.
2. Tape a comb over the hole.
3. Hold the card stock upright on a table and turn off the lights in the room.
4. Shine a flashlight through the hole, opposite the comb. What happens to the light?
5. Take off the tape. Hold the comb at varying distances from the hole. What do you notice about the light now? Are the lines wider? Shorter? Lighter? Use your science notebook to record your observations. You may also want to draw what you see to show the comparisons.

Move the comb closer to and farther from the hole in the card stock.

BEAUTIFUL PATTERNS

When light hits an object, any of four things can happen. If the object is transparent (see-through), light passes through it. Dark (opaque) objects absorb light. Shiny objects reflect light (they make it bounce back). Some objects will make light bend, which is called refraction.

When light reflects off your body, people can see you. The clothes you wear and your skin reflect light in a random way. When you stand in front of a mirror, some of that light travels in a straight line directly to the mirror. Light rays go through the glass and bounce off the polished surface at the back of the mirror. This reflection is more organized than the reflection of light that usually bounces off your body. That order is what makes it possible to see yourself clearly in the mirror.

If you could watch a ray of light as it approaches and is then reflected off a mirror, you would see that light moves in a predictable way. The diagram illustrates the law of reflection.

The ray of light that approaches the mirror is called

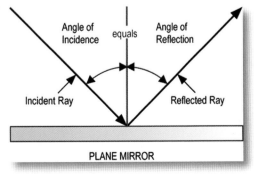

the incident ray. The ray of light that leaves the mirror is called the reflected ray. At the point where the ray hits the mirror, an imaginary perpendicular line, called the normal, can be drawn. The angle between the incident ray and the normal is called the angle of incidence. The angle between the normal and the ray of reflection is called the angle of reflection. According to the law of reflection, the angle of incidence is equal to the angle of reflection.

When two or more mirrors are placed next to each other, you see more than one reflection. The light bounces back and forth between the mirrors and the object being reflected. Kaleidoscopes take advantage of this and use it to create colorful patterns. In this activity, you'll use three mirrors to create your own kaleidoscope.

Materials

- Three small rectangular mirrors (available in the hair care section of drugstores or department stores or through science supply catalogs)
- Electrical or duct tape
- Dark-colored card stock
- Pencil
- Scissors
- Tracing paper
- Beads of various colors
- Flashlight

Instructions
1. Tape three small mirrors together to form a triangular prism. The shiny sides should face in.
2. Stand the prism of mirrors up on top of a piece of card stock. Trace around the triangular base, and cut out the shape.

Three taped mirrors

Trace the base of the prism onto card stock.

3. Punch a hole in the center of the card stock base with scissors or a pencil.

4. Tape the base to one end of the triangle of mirrors.

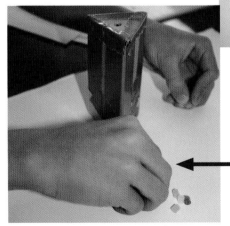

5. Tape tracing paper to the other end of your mirror triangle.

6. Pop a few beads through the hole in the card stock.

7. Shine a flashlight up through the tracing paper and look through the hole in the card stock. Move the kaleidoscope around to change the pattern of beads.

As you twist the kaleidoscope, the beads and their reflections will make new patterns.

More about Mirrors

Not all mirrors are flat. Some are curved. Mirrors that curve inward are called concave. Those that curve outward are called convex. Reflections from curved mirrors look different than those from flat mirrors. You can see this difference by looking at yourself in a spoon.

The front of the spoon is like a concave mirror. Your reflection will look upside down. If you bring the spoon very close to your face, you'll see a large and distorted image but right-side up.

The convex back of the spoon reflects differently. From a distance, your image will be right-side up, but very small. Try this yourself, then experiment with mirrors of different shapes and sizes.

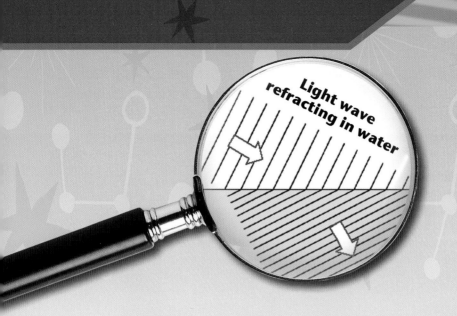

Light wave refracting in water

REFRACTING LIGHT

In a vacuum, light travels at about 186,000 miles per second (300,000 kilometers per second). Light can travel at about that speed in air. When it travels through water or glass, though, it slows down. When light travels from air to water or glass and hits it at an angle, it bends. This is called refraction.

Refraction makes things look like they are cut or bent when parts are above water and parts are below. The next time you are in a swimming pool, look down at your legs. They will look shorter than they really are. Look at the vase with the flower. The stem looks like it has been cut right at the water line. This optical illusion—something that appears to be what it is not—can be taken a step further by completely submerging the object. Its image will be reflected and refracted.

You can experiment with optical illusions by placing objects completely underwater. Draw a picture of what you think the item will look like from the side when it is in the water. Then draw a picture of what it really looks like.

Refraction and Internal Reflection

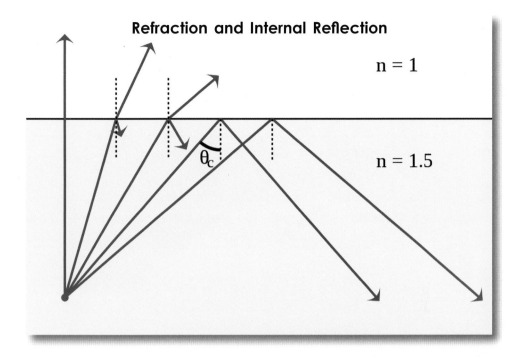

$n = 1$

θ_c

$n = 1.5$

Materials
- Glass bowl
- Small object like a marble or penny (it should not float)
- Water
- Straw or pencil

Can you make a marble appear to float?

Instructions
1. Place a small object inside glass bowl.
2. Pour water into the bowl until the object is submerged (completely underwater).
3. Look at the bowl from the side. You should see an extra "floating" object.

The pencil looks bent when it is partly underwater.

4. Now take the object out of the bowl and let the water settle back down.
5. Gently put a straw or pencil into the water, watching from the side.
6. Notice that the straw or pencil seems to bend as it enters the water. The refraction of light causes these optical illusions.

Antony van Leeuwenhoek

WATER BOTTLE MICROSCOPE

In the last activity, you saw how refracted light can seem to bend or break. Refracted light rays can also make objects seem closer or farther than they really are. Lenses are used to make things seem closer, like those in a telescope. They are also used to make things seem bigger, like those in a microscope. Lenses have one or two curved surfaces. Like curved mirrors, some lenses are concave and some are convex. Concave lenses curve inward. Convex lenses curve outward.

Antony van Leeuwenhoek (1632–1723) became interested in magnifying glasses when he worked in a dry goods store in Holland (The Netherlands). He studied the fibers of fabric underneath them. He became so interested that he began making his own lenses by grinding and polishing glass. He was able to make really small lenses with large curvatures, and his early microscopes could magnify things up to 270 times. He used

Antony van Leeuwenhoek's microscope

this new tool to study bacteria, blood, and tiny organisms in drops of water.

Today, microscopes range from tiny pocket scopes to powerful electron microscopes. In this activity, you will use a plastic water bottle and a drop of water to make your own microscope. The water drop in this simple microscope acts like a convex lens. Light is reflected by the mirror and then is magnified as it passes through the water.

Materials
- Clear plastic water bottle (500 ml, or 16.9 ounces)
- Scissors
- Water
- Small flat mirror
- Small object

Instructions
1. Cut the top off a plastic water bottle.
2. Cut two strips out of the side of the bottle, opposite each other, and each about 1 inch wide and 5 inches long.

Carefully cut a plastic water bottle as shown.

3. Cut two new slits in the side of the bottle, directly across from each other. They should be wide enough to slide the strips through.

4. Insert the end of one of the strips into the slits so that it makes a bridge across the bottle.

5. Place a drop of water in the middle of the strip.

6. Put the mirror under the bottle, facing up.

7. Use the other strip as a slide to hold the object. Hold it underneath the water drop. The object should appear magnified.

Mirror →

Strip with water drop

MAKE YOUR OWN PERISCOPE

As you discovered in the last activity, microscopes use mirrors to reflect light, and they use lenses to magnify the image. Other types of scopes use mirrors and lenses, too. Reflection and refraction are both used to create powerful scopes.

Refracting telescopes work just like eyeglasses do. Light comes in one end of the telescope and is magnified as it passes through the lenses on its way to the observer's eye. Because light travels in a straight path from the object to the eye, refracting scopes tend to cost less than reflecting scopes.

Reflecting telescopes work differently. Light bounces through a series of mirrors inside the tube until it reaches the observer's eye.

Reflection can also be used to see things that are around corners. A periscope uses two mirrors to see around walls and other obstacles. The captain of a submarine can use a periscope to look in all directions above the surface of the water, even when the sub is completely submerged. Interestingly, the word *periscope* comes from two Greek words: *Peri* means "around," and *scopus* means "to look," so *periscope* means "to look around."

Periscopes work because of the law of reflection (see page 12). If a mirror is arranged at a 45-degree angle to the incoming light, the light will bounce off at a 45-degree angle to the second mirror. That mirror reflects the light at the same angle—right into your eyes. Use this simple milk carton periscope to test the law of reflection. You'll be able to see what is going on around your house without being seen.

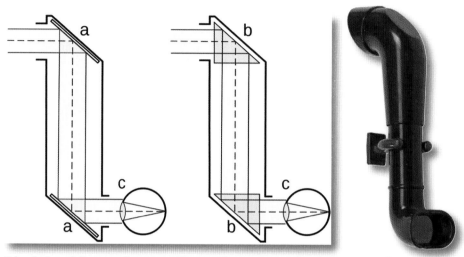

Principle of the periscope. The periscope on the left uses mirrors at location "a"; the one on the right uses prisms at "b." The observer is "c."

Materials
- 2 empty quart-size milk or juice cartons
- Duct tape
- Spray paint (optional) with newspapers and **adult** help
- Protractor
- Ruler
- Marker
- Scissors
- 2 rectangular mirrors, slightly longer than the width of the milk carton

Instructions

1. Rinse and dry the quart-sized containers.
2. Cut off the top of both containers. Use duct tape to tape the two open ends together.
3. If you want, and **under adult supervision**, spray paint the containers, giving them plenty of time to dry before moving on to step 4. (You may want to do this the day before you make your periscope. Be sure to cover any surfaces with newspaper before you paint.)

4. Using a ruler, draw two 45-degree lines on one side of the carton—one near each end of the periscope. Cut each line, making a slot.
5. Turn the carton around and draw two more 45-degree lines, directly opposite the slots on the other side. Cut those out.
6. Push a mirror through each set of slots. The top mirror should be shiny-side down. The bottom mirror should be shiny-side up.
7. Using a ruler, draw a large rectangle in front of the top mirror. Cut it out.
8. Make a small hole with the scissors in the back of the carton, across from the bottom mirror.

Slide mirrors in the slots, facing each other.

9. Look through the hole in your periscope to see around corners and over walls.

What's happening around the corner?

SEPARATING COLORS OF THE SPECTRUM

The electromagnetic spectrum is the range of energy that contains visible light—the light we can see. Have you ever seen a rainbow? The colors that make up that arc in the sky are the same ones that make up the range of visible light. They can be remembered by this name: Roy G. Biv (Red, Orange, Yellow, Green, Blue, Indigo, Violet). Each color has its own wavelength. When these colors are blended together, they make white light.

Outside the range of visible light are other wavelengths of electromagnetic energy. Although we cannot see them, we can feel some of them. Infrared ("below red") light can warm us. Ultraviolet ("beyond violet") light can burn us if we forget to wear sunscreen on a

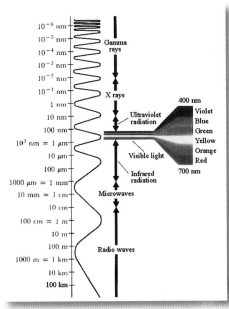

summer day. Microwaves are longer than infrared waves, and radio waves are longer than microwaves. In the other direction, far beyond ultraviolet, are X-rays and gamma rays.

Each wavelength of light travels at a different speed. This makes it possible to separate white light into all of its colors. In this activity, you'll use water as a prism to separate the different wavelengths that make up white light. A prism separates light using refraction. When light enters the glass, it slows down. It speeds back up as it leaves the glass. Because the colors have different wavelengths, they are refracted at different angles. You end up with a rainbow.

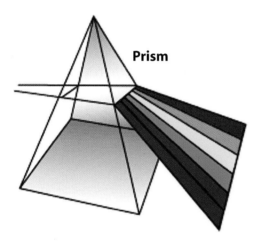

Prism

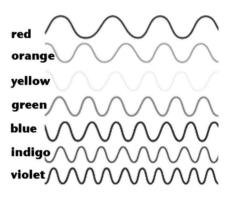

red
orange
yellow
green
blue
indigo
violet

Instructions

1. On a sunny day, fill a tray with water and set it near a sunny window. Let the water settle.
2. Place a mirror at an angle in the tray so that the light from the window hits it. **NEVER LOOK DIRECTLY AT THE SUN OR ITS REFLECTION.**
3. Hold a piece of card stock in front of the mirror, moving it around until you see a rainbow appear. NOTE: You may have to move the mirror a bit as well to get the angles just right.

Materials
- Tray, 2 inches deep
- Water
- Mirror
- Sunny window
- White card stock

Small glass and plastic prisms are widely available at craft stores, toy stores, and science or teacher supply stores and catalogs for a few

Use a tray of water and a mirror to make a rainbow.

dollars each. You may want to purchase one and separate the light from various sources around your house. Try holding it beneath a bedside lamp. Experiment to see if there is a difference when you hold it near the kitchen chandelier or the bathroom light. What colors do you see? Are they always in the same order?

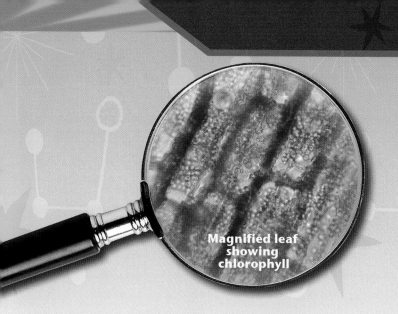

Magnified leaf showing chlorophyll

SUNLIGHT AND PLANTS

The sun gives us heat energy and light energy in many wavelengths of light, including ultraviolet (UV) radiation. "UV radiation" covers a range of wavelengths. The shorter the wavelength, the more harm the radiation can cause. On Earth, we deal with both the harmful and the helpful effects of UV radiation. Plants use it to grow. People get sunburned from it.

Plants use energy from the sun in order to make food. If you look closely at a field of flowers in bloom, you will see that they all face the same way—toward the sun.

Plants trap UV radiation using the green chlorophyll in their leaves. During photosynthesis, this sunlight is used to convert nutrients from the soil into food. (The word *photo* means "light.") When a plant's leaves are covered, sunlight cannot be absorbed. If

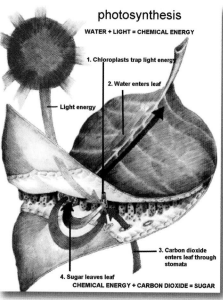

photosynthesis
WATER + LIGHT = CHEMICAL ENERGY

1. Chloroplasts trap light energy

2. Water enters leaf

Light energy

3. Carbon dioxide enters leaf through stomata

4. Sugar leaves leaf
CHEMICAL ENERGY + CARBON DIOXIDE = SUGAR

sunlight can't be absorbed, the plant cannot make food, and it will not survive.

See the effects of sunlight on plants yourself in this activity. You'll see how plants grow when sunlight reaches them directly, when it cannot reach them at all, and when it is just out of the way. Be patient. This activity will take a week or longer.

Materials
- Scissors
- Shoebox (or other type of box) with lid
- Plastic wrap
- Paper towels
- Water
- Cardboard
- Tape
- Cress seeds
- Sunny window

Instructions

1. Cut an opening out of one end of a shoebox.

2. Line the bottom of the box with plastic wrap.

3. Place paper towels over the plastic wrap and dampen them with water.

4. Cut off one third of the box lid.

5. Cut two pieces from a sheet of cardboard to fit, standing up, inside the box. Tape them in place so that they divide the box into three sections.

6. Scatter cress seeds on the dampened paper towels in all three sections of the box. Try to do this evenly throughout the box.

7. Put the lid on the box. The section with the cutout opening and the middle section should be covered.

Use damp paper towels.

Scatter seeds evenly.

8. Place the box in a sunny window. Water your seeds daily for a week.

9. After the week is up, or when you see plants with leaves, remove the lid and look at your plants. Plants in each section should have grown very differently. How did the sunlight affect each section?

How did the plants grow in each section?

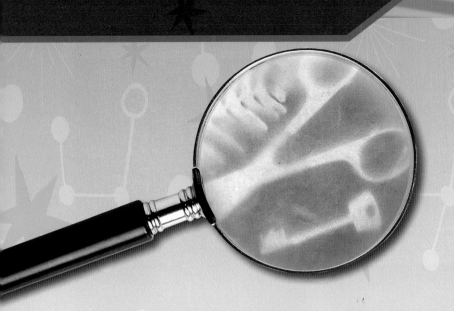

SUNSCREEN STRENGTH

In the last activity, you experimented with the helpful effects of ultraviolet (UV) radiation. Short-wave UV radiation is responsible for causing sunburns. Ozone and other gases in Earth's atmosphere stop most UV rays before they get to us. That's a good thing—if too much UV light made it through the atmosphere, Earth would get too hot for life as we know it.

Still, the small amount of UV light that makes it through can cause us harm. It is important for people to wear sunscreen when they are outside on sunny days. In this activity, you'll test the effects of different brands or strengths of sunscreen to see which is most effective. You may be surprised at your results.

Materials
- Five sheets of sun print paper (available at craft stores)
- Five clear plastic bags, large enough to hold a full sheet of sun print paper
- Permanent marker
- Four different brands or strengths of sunscreen
- Tub of water

Instructions

1. Decide if you want to test different brands or different strengths of sunscreen. If you choose to test different brands, buy four different bottles of sunscreen, each made by a different company. Make sure they are all the same strength. If you choose to test the same brand, buy four bottles of sunscreen, each a different strength but made by the same brand.
2. Work in an area that is far away from a window so that you don't expose the sun paper to the sunlight too soon.
3. Use a permanent marker to label each sheet of paper with the type of sunscreen. One will be your control sheet—label it Control.
4. Place each sheet of sun paper into a different bag.
5. Spread the entire front of each bag with the type of sunscreen written on it. Leave the control bag free of sunscreen. (NOTE: Make sure you spread the sunscreen on the side of the bag that exposes the part of the paper that will turn blue.)
6. Lay the bags in the sun, with sunscreen up, for five minutes.
7. Remove each sheet of paper from its bag.

By using a control, you will know how the sun paper would look with no sunscreen at all.

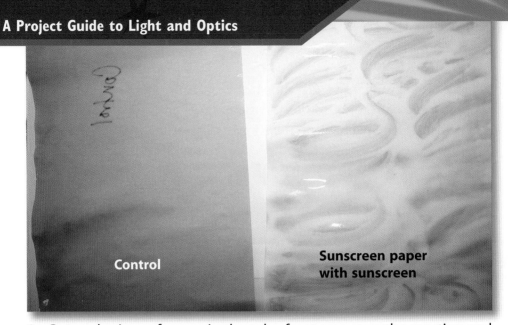

Control

Sunscreen paper with sunscreen

8. Put each piece of paper in the tub of water to stop the reaction and fix the "image."
9. Spread them out side by side. The bluer the paper is, the more ultraviolet light passed through the sunscreen. The paper that was blocked by the strongest sunscreen should be mostly white. The control paper should be all blue.

More to Do with Sun Paper

It is fun to make shadow pictures with ultraviolet light. Lay small objects, such as letters, a comb, or whatever else you want to make on the sun paper, then expose it to the sun for 2 to 4 minutes. Rinse the paper to fix the image. Now you have some cool new artwork to hang in your room, all made by the power of sunlight.

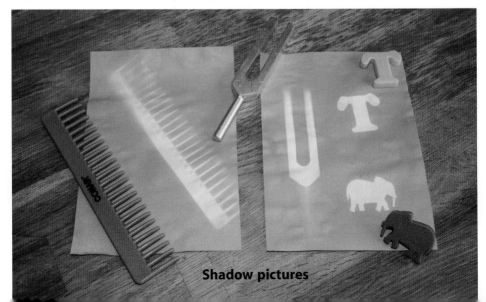

Shadow pictures

DIFFERENT LIGHT SOURCES

Most light that you see is incoherent light. It has many wavelengths, and the rays spread out as they travel.

Light that is made up of only one wavelength is called coherent light. Lasers produce a narrow and intense beam of concentrated light that is coherent. The highly concentrated beam of light energy in high-powered lasers can cut or drill objects.

In this activity, you will compare the beams from a coherent and an incoherent light source.

Materials
- Room that can be darkened
- Tape measure
- Masking tape
- Flashlight
- Friend
- Paper and pencil
- Laser pointer

NEVER POINT A LASER AT SOMEONE'S EYES.

Instructions

1. Find a room that can get very dark when the lights are off. Measure three feet away from a wall in that room, and tape a line to the floor.
2. Measure and mark 6 and 9 feet from the wall, too.

Use tape to mark distances from the wall.

3. Turn off the lights, stand on the first line facing the wall, and shine the flashlight on the wall.
4. Ask your friend to measure the diameter of the light beam on the wall. Record the measurement.

3 feet

6 feet

5. Move back to the 6-foot line. Have your friend measure and record the diameter again.
6. Repeat this at the 9-foot line.
7. Go back to the first line. Repeat steps 3-6 with the laser pointer.
8. Talk to your friend about your results. What happened as you moved the flashlight beam farther from the wall? What happened when you moved the laser pointer farther from the wall? How did the beams differ?

Compare a laser beam to a flashlight beam.

Will a laser beam spread out like a flashlight beam?

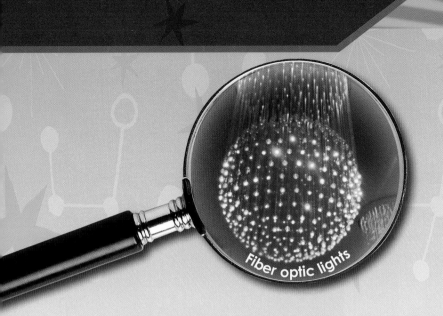
Fiber optic lights

STREAMING LIGHT

Fiber optics uses the laws of reflection and refraction to transport light in a very direct way. Pulses of light (either ultraviolet light or laser light) are sent through a small glass fiber about the diameter of a human hair. The fiber is in a cladding, which keeps the light from escaping the glass. Each pulse is reflected back and forth along the glass until it reaches a receiver at the other end of the fiber. (This is called total internal reflection.) The receiver translates the pulses into electrical signals.

Fiber optics is important because it allows us to send information very quickly. Sound and images can be transferred using these pulses of light.

This activity will show you how light can follow the path of optic fibers, even when they are bent. You will use water as your fiber.

Materials	Scissors
An adult	Safety pin
Plastic water bottle	Glass dish
Black paint	Water
Old newspapers	Flashlight

Be sure to cover surfaces with old newspaper before you paint.

Instructions

1. **Under adult supervision**, paint a water bottle black and let it dry.
2. Take the lid off the bottle.
3. Use a pin to poke a hole about a third of the way up the bottle.
4. Directly opposite the pinhole, scrape away a small amount of paint.
5. Set the bottle in a glass dish and turn the lights off in the room.

Put everything in one place before you turn off the lights.

Light will follow a stream of water, just as it will follow a glass fiber.

6. Fill the bottle three-quarters full of water, and shine the flashlight through the area you scraped clean.
7. Place your finger directly in the water stream. You should be able to see a spot of light on your finger.

The water stream acts like glass fiber from a fiber optic cable. The light bounces back and forth along the water stream until it hits your finger. The concentrated beam shows up as a spot on your finger.

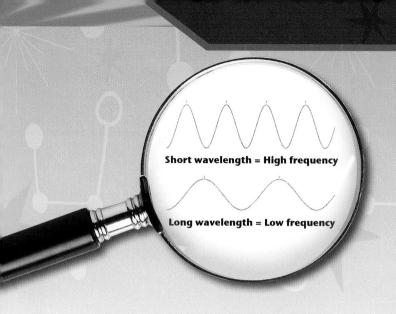

Short wavelength = High frequency

Long wavelength = Low frequency

MEASURING THE SPEED OF LIGHT

Albert Einstein was reportedly interested in light from the time he was a young boy. At sixteen years old, he wondered what it would be like to ride on a beam of light. As he grew older, he questioned the theories of his day about light. He believed that light traveled at a constant speed, but only in a vacuum. It would slow down or speed up in various substances.

In the early 1900s, he wrote several groundbreaking papers. They changed the way people understood light and energy. One of his papers showed how energy (E), mass (m), and the speed of light (c) are related. His equation became famous: $E = mc^2$.

How is it possible to measure the speed of light? Microwave is a type of light wave from the "invisible" part of the electromagnetic spectrum. In this activity, you will use a microwave and other normal (and delicious!) household materials to measure just how fast light actually travels. It's okay to eat the product of this experiment.

Materials
- Microwave-safe dish
- Large marshmallows
- Microwave oven
- Metric ruler
- Calculator

Instructions

1. Place a single layer of marshmallows across the entire surface of a microwave-safe dish.
2. Remove the turntable inside your microwave oven, if it has one, or set the microwave to Turntable Off. You do not want the dish to turn.
3. Place the dish in the center of the microwave floor. Cook the marshmallows on low until there are four to six "hot spots" where the marshmallows are melted.
4. Pull the dish out of the microwave. Be careful! It might be hot. Microwaves don't cook evenly, so when you pull the dish out, you should see several concentrated melted spots.
5. Use a metric ruler to measure the distance between the spots. NOTE: For accuracy in this activity, measure the distance between each of the spots, add up the measurements, and divide the sum by the number of measurements you added together. This will give you the average distance between spots.
6. The distance you just measured is half of one microwave wavelength. Double that measurement to get the value of one wavelength.
7. Find the frequency at which your microwave operates. It is usually written on a sticker on the back or side of the microwave. Most standard microwaves operate at a frequency of 2,450 MHz (which is the same as 2,450,000,000 hertz). A hertz is one cycle per second.
8. You now have all the numbers you need to calculate the speed of light. Use them in this formula: velocity = frequency x wavelength.
9. Multiply frequency (2,450,000,000 Hz, or the number you found on your microwave) by the wavelength (your doubled measurement between hot spots). Since the wavelength was measured in

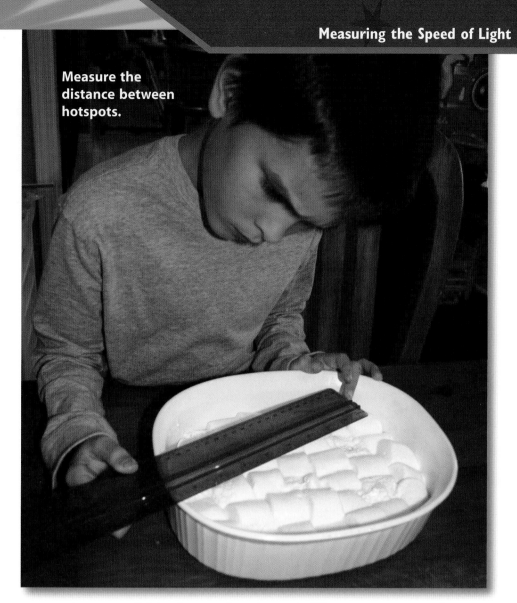

Measure the distance between hotspots.

centimeters, divide the product by 100. (There are 100 centimeters in a meter, and the speed of light is usually given in meters or kilometers per second).

What did you get? Your answer should be pretty close to the speed of light (299,742,458 meters per second). Because the marshmallows stayed still in the microwave, the wave continued to hit them in the same places. These spots melted, while the other spots remained unchanged. The distance between each melted spot is one-half a wavelength, since the waves passed through the marshmallows on their way up and on their way down.

Books

Dispezio, Michael A., and Rob Collinet. *Awesome Experiments in Light and Sound.* New York: Sterling Publishers, 2006.

Jackson, Tom. *Experiments with Light and Color.* New York: Gareth Stevens, 2010.

Pasachoff, Jay M. *Prentice Hall Science Explorer.* Upper Saddle River, NJ: Pearson/Prentice Hall, 2007.

Sohn, Emily, and Nick Derington. *The Illuminating World of Light with Max Axiom, Super Scientist.* Mankato, MN: Capstone, 2007.

Works Consulted

The Astronomical Society of New South Wales, Inc. "Ancient Egyptian Optics." *Alternate Universe.* Accessed November 14, 2010. http://www.asnsw.com/universe/alternate/AU9/egyptianoptics.asp

Blair, William P. "The Basics of Light." *Far Ultraviolet Spectroscopic Explorer,* March 2004. Accessed October 30, 2010. http://fuse.pha.jhu.edu/~wpb/spectroscopy/basics.html

Brox, Jane. *Brilliant: The Evolution of Artificial Light.* Boston: Houghton Mifflin Harcourt, 2010.

Conlan, Roberta, and T. A. Heppenheimer. "Modern Communication: The Laser and Fiber Optic Revolution." *Beyond Discovery, National Academy of Sciences,* December 1996. Accessed October 30, 2010. http://www.beyonddiscovery.org/includes/DBFile.asp?ID=90

"Fiber Optics." OSA Foundation. Optical Society of America. Accessed November 8, 2010. http://www.osa-foundation.org/FiberOpticsPamphlet

Fowles, Grant R. *Introduction to Modern Optics.* New York: Dover Publications, 1989.

Hulst, Hendrik. *Light Scattering by Small Particles.* New York: Dover, 2009.

Kirkland, Kyle. *Light and Optics.* New York: Facts on File, 2007.

"Laser Light Proves to Have Many Uses in Business, Health, Communications." *Washingtonpost.com*, January 19, 2010. Accessed October 28, 2010. http://www.washingtonpost.com/wp-dyn/content/article/2010/01/15/AR2010011503122.html.

NOVA: "Einstein's Big Idea." PBS: Public Broadcasting Service. Accessed November 8, 2010. http://www.pbs.org/wgbh/nova/einstein/

Optical Society of America: Exploring the Science of Light—"Optics Timeline." Accessed November 8, 2010. http://www.optics4kids.com/opticstimeline/

On the Internet

The NASA Science Files Kids: Light and Color
http://scifiles.larc.nasa.gov/kids/Problem_Board/problems/light/
sim1.html
Optical Research Associates
http://www.opticalres.com/kidoptx_f.html
Optical Society of America: Exploring the Science of Light
http://www.optics4kids.com/
Physics 4 Kids
http://www.physics4kids.com/files/light_intro.html
Science, Optics, and You
http://www.molecularexpressions.com/optics/activities/students/
index.html

Science Supply Companies

Edmund Scientifics
http://www.scientificsonline.com/
Educational Innovations
http://www.teachersource.com/LightAndColor.aspx
Science Kit & Boreal Laboratories
http://sciencekit.com/Default.asp?bhcd2=1258230685
Science Kit Store
http://sciencekitstore.com/
Steve Spangler Science Store
http://www.stevespanglerscience.com/

chlorophyll (KLOR-uh-fil)—The green coloring in plants that converts sunlight into chemical energy (food for the plant).

coherent (koh-HEER-ent) **light**—Light made up of wavelengths moving in a uniform way.

concave (kon-KAYV) **lens**—A lens that is thinner in the center than at the edges.

convex (kon-VEKS) **lens**—A lens that is thicker in the center than at the edges.

electromagnetic spectrum (ee-LEK-troh-mag-NEH-tik SPEK-trum)—The range of waves that can transmit energy from one object to another. This energy can be in any of several forms, including light, heat, and sound.

electromagnetism (ee-LEK-troh-MAG-neh-tizm)—Magnetism produced by an electric current.

fiber optics (FY-ber OP-tiks)—Thin, clear glass fibers, enclosed in another material, that carry light along their length by total internal reflection.

incoherent (IN-koh-heer-ent) **light**—Light that spreads out.

laser (LAY-zer)—Light Amplification by Stimulated Emission of Radiation; a device used for making a concentrated beam of coherent light.

lens—A device that can focus or scatter rays of light.

light speed—The speed at which light can travel in a vacuum: approximately 186,000 miles per second, or 300,000 kilometers per second.

microscope (MY-kroh-skohp)—An instrument that uses light, mirrors, and lenses to magnify objects.

mirror—A polished surface that reflects images.

optics—The study of light.

photon (FOH-tahn)—A tiny particle of light.

photosynthesis (foh-toh-SIN-theh-sis)—The process by which plants use sunlight to change carbon dioxide into sugar (food).

prism—A clear object with a flat polished surface that can refract light.

ray—A beam or straight line.

reflection (ree-FLEK-shun)—A ray of light that has been bounced off a surface.

refraction (ree-FRAK-shun)—The turning or bending of a ray of light.

ultraviolet (ul-truh-VY-uh-let) **light**—Light that has a wavelength shorter than visible light but longer than X-rays.

vacuum (VAK-yoom)—A space completely without matter.

visible (VIH-zih-bul) **light**—The range of wavelengths humans can see.

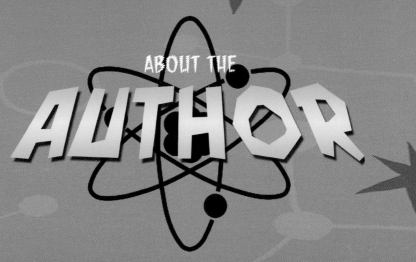

Colleen Kessler is the author of many science books for kids, including *A Project Guide to Reptiles and Birds*, *A Project Guide to the Solar System*, *A Project Guide to Forces and Motion*, and *A Project Guide to Electricity and Magnetism* for Mitchell Lane Publishers. A former teacher of gifted students, Colleen now satisfies her curiosity as a full-time nonfiction writer. She does her researching and writing in her home office overlooking a wooded backyard in Northeastern Ohio. You can often find her blasting off rockets or searching for salamanders with her husband, Brian, and kids, Trevor, Molly, and Logan, or talking to schoolchildren about the excitement of studying science and nature. For more information about her books and presentations, or to invite her for a school visit, check out her website at http://www.colleen-kessler.com.